Contents and Projects pages 4 - 21

Using Polymer Clay
pages 4 - 5

Zentangle®
pages 6 - 8

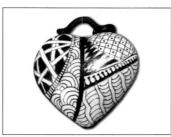

Heart Pendant
pages 9 - 10

Carved Bangle Bracelet
pages 11 - 12

Etched Earrings
pages 12 - 13

Carved Pin
pages 14 - 15

Mirror Frame
pages 16 - 17

Silk Screened Bracelet
pages 18 - 21

Canes and Projects pages 22 - 51

#1
26 - 27

#2
28

#3
29

#4
30

#5
31

#6
32 - 33

#7
34 - 35

#8

#9

#11
39

Decorated Sheets
pages 40 - 41

Big Beads
pages 42 - 43

Pillow Beads
pages 44 - 45

Trinket Box
pages 46 - 49

Big Big Beads
pages 50 - 51

Using Polymer Clay

Basic Clay Supplies

Polymer Clay (For caning the stiffer brands work better. Try Kato, Premo or Fimo Classic) • Pasta Machine (For conditioning the clay) • Work surface (ceramic tile or glass) • Acrylic rod or brayer • Clay blade for slicing

Types of Clay

There are several brands of polymer clay on the market. Some are more suited for canework than others. When making canes, it is better to use stiffer clays such as Kato, Premo or Fimo Classic. Sculpey III is too soft and not recommended for caning, but it works well if you draw your tangle patterns on the clay.

Helpful Tools

Needle tools • Small paintbrushes • Ruler • Ceramic tile • Cyanoacrylate glue • Clay shape cutter • Small drills • Burnishing tools such as a door knob

Additional Supplies

Liquid Clay • ArmorAll • Deli wrap or plastic wrap • Heavy Weight Cardstock • Wet/Dry Sandpaper 220, 400, 600, 800 and 1000 grit • Hair curler for texturizing clay

Tip: There are two kinds of deli wrap that I use with my polymer clay. The first is a clear plastic wrap. I use this to wrap my canes and extra clay. It comes in a green box and is made by Papercon. You can also use regular plastic wrap that you get at a grocery store. One advantage that the Papercon wrap has is that it is better for smoothing your clay.

Place a wrinkle-free piece of wrap over your clay and use a burnisher or your fingers to smooth out any fingerprints or imperfections. Regular plastic wrap tends to wrinkle, which adds problems instead of reducing them. The other Papercon wrap that I use is called delicatessen paper and comes in a red box. This is more like wax paper, only thinner. I use this also to smooth out my clay and to store my decorated sheets. You can also use parchment paper for smoothing your clay, but don't use it to store your clay.

... inspired by Zentangle

Conditioning the Clay

Before you can use polymer clay, you must condition it. Conditioning makes the clay strong when baked. It is important to condition the clay even if it feels soft right out of the package. This means working the clay, either with your hands or with a pasta machine, until it is soft and pliable. Once you use a pasta machine for clay, it cannot be used for food.

To condition clay without a pasta machine, take a slice off the block of clay and roll it between your palms. As it warms up, fold the clay onto itself and roll some more. Keep repeating this until the clay becomes soft and malleable.

   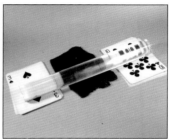

A pasta machine for clay is a useful tool. Follow the manufacturer's instructions for determining settings. • If you don't have a pasta machine, use an acrylic rod to flatten and condition the clay. • The thickest setting on a pasta machine is usually $1/8$" - $1/4$". • Use your acrylic rod to flatten out the clay. To achieve a uniform thickness, without the use of a pasta machine, stack regular playing cards equally on either side of the clay. The height of the stack will determine the thickness of the clay sheet. Place the flattened clay between the two stacks of cards. Roll the acrylic roller over the clay until the roller touches the top cards. If you need a thinner sheet, just remove cards from both stacks and roll again.

   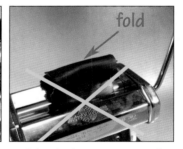

To condition clay using the pasta machine, cut a slice that is slightly less than twice the thickness of the thickest setting on the pasta machine. Put it on your work surface and use an acrylic rod to flatten it slightly. • Use a blade to scrape it off the work surface. • Roll it through the pasta machine at the thickest setting. Now dial your pasta machine to the next thinnest setting and feed the sheet through again. Repeat this, reducing the thickness until you are past a medium setting. Now set the pasta machine back to the second thickest setting. • Fold the sheet in half and feed the fold in first. Repeat this step until the clay is conditioned. It may help to turn your clay so the fold is perpendicular to the roller blades every once in a while. • Never position the fold at the top because this can trap air into your clay. Air is not a friend of polymer clay because internal air bubbles expand during the baking process and crack the clay.

Baking the Clay

Polymer clay needs to be baked or cured in an oven or toaster oven. Follow manufacturer's recommendations for the brand of clay that you are using. Just as with the pasta machine, do not use a food oven to bake clay. I purchased an inexpensive toaster oven for exclusive use with clay.

Zentangle®

The History of Zentangle

While drawing background patterns on a manuscript, Maria Thomas experienced "feelings of timelessness, freedom, well-being and complete focus on what she was doing with no thought or worry about anything else." When she described this meditative state to Rick Roberts, they explored the possibilities of sharing this experience with others, and thus, the ritual they call Zentangle® was born.

*Rick and Maria (**zentangle.com**) began teaching workshops and training others to teach Zentangle. Now there are hundreds of CZTs (Certified Zentangle Teachers) around the world, spreading the calm that grows from this relaxing art form. Zentangle® can be done anywhere and no 'artistic' talent is needed. The ritual helps anyone get in touch with life, solve problems, turn mistakes into positives, be innovative and become more creative.*

Learn to create fascinating tangles and enjoy the experience that tangling brings.

You'll find wonderful resources, a list of CZTs, workshops, a fabulous gallery of inspiring projects, supplies, kits, and tiles at zentangle.com.

Traditional Zentangle...

A very simple ritual is part of every traditional Zentangle.

1. Make a dot in each corner of your paper tile or clay shape with a pencil. Connect the dots to form a basic frame.
2. Draw guideline "strings" with the pencil. The shape can be a zigzag, swirl, X, circle or just about anything that divides the area into sections. It represents the "golden thread" that connects all the patterns and events that run through life. The lines will not be erased but become part of the design.
3. Use a black pen to draw Tangle patterns into each section formed by the "string".
4. Rotate the paper tile or clay piece as you fill each section with a pattern.

How to Get Started...

1. Use a pencil to make a dot in each corner.

2. Connect the dots with the pencil.

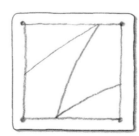

3. Draw a "string" with the pencil as a guide line.
    Try a Z zigzag, a ◌ loop, an X ' X' or a swirl.

4. Switch to a pen and draw tangle patterns into the sections formed by the "string". When you cross a line, change the pattern.

It is OK to leave some sections blank.

Each Tangle is a unique artistic design and there are hundreds of variations. Start with basic patterns, then create your own.

With Zentangle, no eraser is needed. Just as in life, we cannot erase events and mistakes, instead we must build upon them and make improvements from any event.

Life is a building process. All memories, events and experiences are incorporated into our learning process and into our life patterns.

Bead by Bead

Teardrops

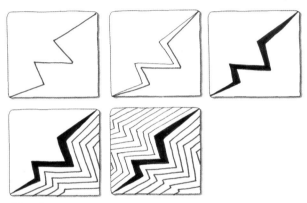

*Static** original Zentangle design - Variation

*Knightsbridge** Variation
original Zentangle design

*Hollibaugh** original Zentangle design - Variation

*Flukes** original Zentangle design

Clay Classics... inspired by Zentangle 7

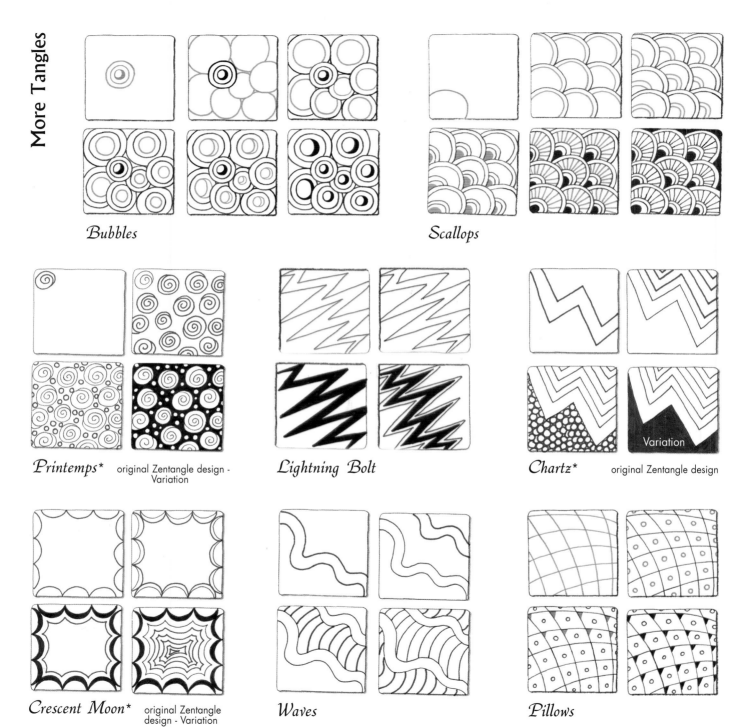

Bubbles

Scallops

*Printemps**   original Zentangle design - Variation

Lightning Bolt

*Chartz**   original Zentangle design

*Crescent Moon**   original Zentangle design - Variation

Waves

Pillows

Heart Pendant

Wear your original Zentangle art piece with pride!

You can make other shapes on which to draw. Try pendants, pins, bracelets or book covers.

For larger objects, you may find it helpful to brush the sealer on sections of the design as you finish them. This will keep the ink from smearing.

Tangle patterns are drawn by hand (see pages 6 - 8)

EXTRA SUPPLIES
Heat gun • 1¹/₂" - 2" Heart cookie cutter
Black permanent ink pens - *Sakura* MICRON 01 is suggested
Sealer made for polymer clay

  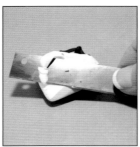  

Stack several sheets of white clay on top of a sheet of black clay. Cut a heart shape or use a cookie cutter to cut the heart.
• Roll with the acrylic rod to remove air from between the sheets. • Shape a black snake and adhere to the top of the heart as a hanger for a necklace. • Use your blade to remove the excess clay from around the heart. Bevel the white clay towards the center of the heart. • Place a small ball of white clay in the center of the white clay and push the clay together. Smooth it out to the edges to form a rounded top on the heart. • Shape the heart by rocking the pendant back and forth on your work surface. You can also use your blade to help shape the heart.

Shape the heart with your fingers. • Brush the heart with cornstarch. Use your fingers to smooth the surface of the heart until you have a nice domed shape. • Place the heart on cardstock and bake following the manufacturer's instructions. Let cool. Sand with 220 grit wet/dry sandpaper.

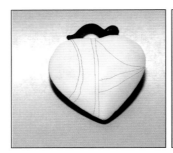

Use a pencil to mark sections (see pages 6 - 7). • Use permanent markers (MICRON black 01 and 08 are suggested) to draw Tangles in one section on the clay heart. • Draw another Tangle pattern in a second section on the heart. • Draw additional Tangle patterns until the design is complete. Allow ink to dry thoroughly. • Use the heat gun to set the ink.

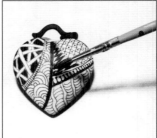

Fill in all of the zones with a different design. Use the heat gun to seal the final design. • Brush on 2-3 coats of sealer on top of the finished Zentangle heart, letting it dry between coats.

Carved Bangle Bracelet

This project will be carved like the Pin on page 14. However, instead of using a thin layer of black, you will fill in the carved out spaces with white clay. This will make your carved design stand out.

EXTRA SUPPLIES
Small 'v' or 'u' shaped
   carving tools
Small drill
Large circle cutter that fits
   your wrist
Sealer made for polymer
   clay

Roll out a 4¹/2" square sheet of Red clay on the thickest setting of your pasta machine. • Roll out 2 thin sheets of black and apply them to each side of the red square. • Start laying the sheet at one end and press towards the other side. Do not trap air between the layers. • Use an acrylic roller to seal all of the layers. • Using a large circle cutter, cut out the center of the bangle bracelet. continued on page 12

Carved Bangle Bracelet continue from page 11

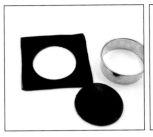 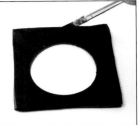 

Use a craft knife to cut out a freeform outer shape for your bangle. Place the bangle between two sheets of cardstock and bake following the manufacturer's instructions. Remove from the oven. If the bangle has started to curl, place a book on top of the cardstock and bangle while the piece is still warm. Let cool. Sand the bracelet with 220 grit wet/dry sandpaper.

Mark sections using a white pencil. • Carve a design into each segment. • To fill the lines, you need some conditioned white clay. If your clay is dry, add a small amount of Liquid Clay. Continue to condition the clay. Use your finger to spread the white clay into the carved out lines. Use your clay blade to remove excess clay.

You will be sanding once the bangle is baked but it is easier to remove the excess now, than to sand later. Fill all the lines. Bake the bangle on a piece of cardstock. Let cool. • Sand off the excess clay. Begin with 220 grit wet/dry sandpaper. Continue with 400, 600 and 800 grit sandpaper. Repeat for the other side of the bangle bracelet. If needed, re-carve, refill any gaps in the design, bake and sand again.

Etched Earrings

You can achieve the look of carved lines by drawing onto the unbaked clay with a needle tool.

EXTRA SUPPLIES
2 ear wires
2 jump rings
White acrylic paint
Circle cutter
Needle tool

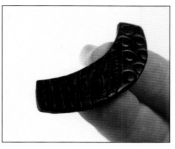

Roll out a sheet of black clay on a medium setting of your pasta machine. Using a circle cutter, cut 2 circles from the clay.
• Use the circle cutter again to make a pair of curved earrings. • Using a needle tool, draw a design directly onto the unbaked clay. • Experiment with other tools that will leave the desired design.

Place the earrings onto cardstock and bake following the manufacturer's instructions. Let cool. • Place a small amount of white paint onto your fingertip. • Use your finger to spread the paint into the grooves of the earring. • Use a paper towel to remove the excess paint from the surface.

Place the earrings on cardstock and bake in the oven for 5 minutes. Let cool. • Use 220 grit sandpaper to remove any paint from the surface of the earring. • Sand across the top surface only so that the white paint remains in the etched grooves.
• Drill holes into the earrings. Attach ear wires with jump rings.

Carved Pin

For this project we will carve a design on a formed surface. To reduce the weight of the large pin, use Ultralight clay for the base. Ultralight clay resembles marshmallows and is much lighter than regular polymer clay.

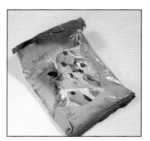 

EXTRA SUPPLIES
Sculpey Ultralight clay
Small 'v' or 'u' shaped carving tools
Small drill
Pin back

Tip: Before carving your first pin, bake some scrap clay and practice carving. Hold the carving tool with the sharp tip pointing away from you. The tips are very sharp and if you slip, you don't want to cut your hand. Work slowly and with equal pressure. When you are ready to make a curve, turn the piece instead of the tool. It's easy to carve too deep so observe the amount of clay being cut away and keep it smaller than your carving tip so you get a clean cut.

Also, when you are just starting out, it's easier to carve on a flat surface. Try curved surfaces when you have more experience carving the clay.

   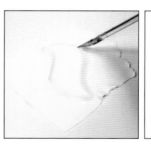 

Using Ultralight clay, make a freeform shape with a flat top surface. Bake following the manufacturer's instructions. Let cool. If there are rough spots on the piece, use sandpaper to smooth them. • Apply a small amount of Liquid Clay to the top of the shape. • Roll out a sheet of white clay on a medium setting of the pasta machine. Place this over the base pin and use a knife to cut away the excess. Apply some Liquid Clay to the back of the base pin. • Roll out a sheet of black clay on a medium setting. Place the pin on the sheet and cut away the excess clay.

Make a stack of clay with 1 thin sheet of black and 2 medium thicknesses of white clay. Do not trap air between the layers. If you see air bubbles, cut into the air hole and squeeze out the air. • A trick for making the top layer of black clay very thin is to run the entire stack through the pasta machine on a medium thickness. You want a thin layer of Black so that when you carve into the baked pin it will not take much to expose the white clay beneath. • Cover the top of the base pin with the thinned sheet and wrap it over the edge.• Use a knife tool to cut away the excess from the back. • You need to cover the back of the pin again because some of the white may show through. Place the pin on top of a thin sheet of black. Cut away the excess.

The top layer of black is very thin so you want as smooth a finish on the pre-baked state as possible. Brush the piece with corn starch. • Use your fingers to rub the piece with corn starch to make it smooth. The baked Ultralight pin is now completely covered with unbaked clay. Use a small sewing needle to poke holes in the piece so air can escape when you bake. In the picture I am using a needle tool for demonstration purposes. You will want to use a thinner sewing needle to make small, inconspicuous holes. Bake the pin again following the manufacturer's instructions. • Use a light colored pencil to mark design segments. • Carve, following the marked lines.

Carve each segment with a different pattern. • You can make small uniform circles using a small drill. • After carving the pin front, apply a little Liquid Clay to the back of the pin. • Position the pin back in the top third of the back. Cover the pin back with a small patch of black clay. Texturize the patch and bake the pin for the final time.

Mirror Frame

I purchased a black frame. If yours isn't black, paint it. While it is drying, gather your design 'tools'.

In this case your design tools will not be pens, pencils or even carving tools, but clay itself.

EXTRA SUPPLIES
Black mirror or frame
Clay extruder
Cyanoacrylate glue
Sealer made for polymer clay
Foam brush
Tweezers

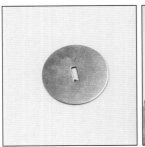

The clay extruder has an assortment of disks. To 'draw' the lines that delineate the tangle segments, use the disk that extrudes a small rectangle. • Place a small amount of conditioned white clay into the barrel of the clay extruder and turn the handle to create a thin flat "line" of clay. Use other disks to make thin lines of clay that can be used for your tangle patterns. • For the larger sized disks, extrude a few inches of clay in the selected shape. • Gather up all of your extruded pieces and place them on cardstock. Bake according to manufacturer's directions. Tip: Polymer clay can be bent into the desired shape if it has been cured properly. If you find that your clay is breaking, it is possible that either you baked it at the incorrect temperature or not long enough. • Glue the segment lines to the frame, one small section at a time.

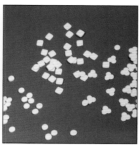

Use a clay blade to cut slices from the baked extruded clay. Cutting before baking distorts the shape. • Now you have a nice collection of slices to use on your frame. • Fill each section with a different design. • Vary your designs, filling some segments with small slices and others with extruded lines. • To shape curved lines, 'warm up' the curve by wrapping the clay around your finger before gluing it to the frame. • When gluing the clay to the frame. take your time and work in a well-ventilated area. Use a pair of tweezers to hold the clay while you apply the glue.

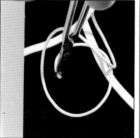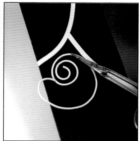

Use tweezers to hold down the clay while it adheres to the frame. • Work a small section at a time. • If your tools get sticky, clean them to avoid picking the clay up when you want it to stay down. You will get excess glue on the frame but the sealer will hide it. • Sometimes it helps to build the design first and then apply it to the frame. For the "woven" segment, tape small lines of unbaked clay to a sheet of cardstock. Weave the line over and under and tape the ends down. Be sure that your design is larger than the segment you plan to fill on your frame. You can press down gently to seal the intersections. Place the cardstock with the taped design into the oven and bake. Let cool. Remove the clay from the cardstock. Dab glue on some of the cross points in the center and place into an empty segment of your frame. Use a craft knife to cut away the excess. Apply more glue as needed. • To make the design in the top left section, extrude small lines of clay. Place the unbaked clay on a piece of cardstock in a random design. Place another sheet of cardstock on top and use an acrylic rod to flatten the design. Pop the cardstock and clay into the oven and bake. The flattened design is easier to glue and can be easily trimmed with a knife tool. Fill in each segment. • Use a foam brush to apply a sealer. Sealer secures the pieces to the frame and covers up any excess glue.

Silk Screened Bracelet

This is a fun way to preserve Zentangle patterns that you have drawn with pen and paper. I scanned mine then used the computer-generated patterns for Silk Screen.

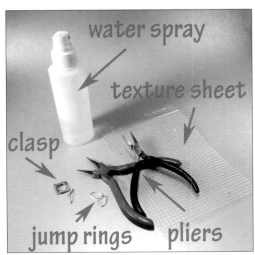

water spray

texture sheet

clasp

jump rings

pliers

EXTRA SUPPLIES
Black and White Zentangle drawing
Silk Screen
2 pieces of glass
Binder Clips
Black felt
Various shape cutters
White paint
Old plastic credit card or gift card
Ceramic tile or glass
Texture plate
Large jump rings
Clasp
Two pairs of jewelry pliers
Spray bottle and water
Heat gun
Small drill
Cyanoacrylate glue

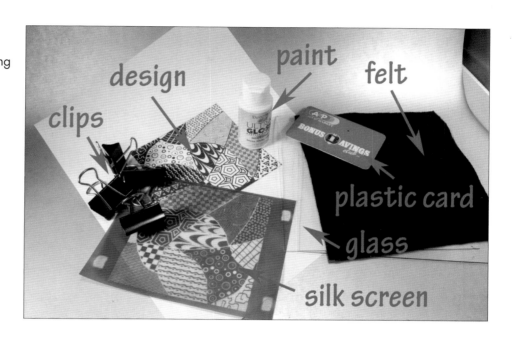

Lay one piece of glass on your work surface. Place black felt on top of the glass. Peel the protective backing from the silk screen sheet. Place the sheet on top of the felt with the shiny side facing up. Lay your black and white design face down. Place the second glass on top of the stack. Use clips to secure around the silk screen. • Follow the manufacturer's instructions for exposing to bright sunlight and washing the polymers off of the silk screen. Let dry before using. You now have a reusable silk screen. • Roll out a sheet of black clay on a medium thickness of your pasta machine. Place the silk screen, shiny side down, on top of the clay. • Apply the paint to the silk screen. • Using the plastic card, spread the paint evenly across the silk screen.

Spread the paint evenly over the entire piece. • Peel off the silk screen from the clay. Wash the paint off of the silk screen. If you want your silk screens to last, you should never let the paint dry on the screens. • Let the paint dry on the clay. Place the silk screened clay on a ceramic tile or glass. Press the clay gently so that the clay adheres to the tile/glass. • Cut circles in the silk screened clay using round cutters. Cut as many shapes as you can from the sheet. Even if you do not use them all at this time you may find a use for them later. Do not remove the excess clay at this time. Place the tile/glass in the oven and bake according to directions for your clay. • When the clay has cooled, slide your blade under the silk screened sheet of clay, releasing the sheet from the tile/glass. • Lift up the excess clay.

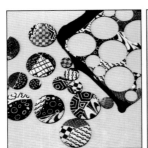

Cut small circles for earrings. • Using a medium setting on the pasta machine, roll out a sheet of red clay. Spritz the red clay with water. • Place a texture plate on top of the red clay and roll the acrylic rod over the texture plate applying consistent pressure. Roll forward only once. • Remove the red clay from the texture plate. • Cut out circles to match the shapes that were cut from the silk screened clay.

Apply the Liquid Clay to the back of one of the baked circles. • Place a red circle on top. • Trim the red circle to fit. • Place the beads on a sheet of cardstock and bake. • Brush each bead with Liquid Clay.

  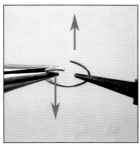  

Place the cured beads on a ceramic tile and heat them with a heat gun. Be sure to keep moving the heat gun at all times. Watch carefully and you will see it turn to a clear shine. • Drill small holes in opposite sides of the bead. • Open one of the jump rings by grasping the ring with two sets of pliers. Rather than pulling the ring open, twist open the ring by turning the ring in opposite directions. • Place two beads on the jump ring and close by reversing the action you used to open the jump ring. • Try to get the ring closed as much as possible. Add a clasp to the end beads.

Cane Making Basics

Making a Cane

So what is a cane? A cane is a log or loaf of clay that has a design running through it so that if you took a cross section anywhere along the log or loaf, the design would be the same.

This technique comes from millefiori glass work in Italy. Millefiori translates into "thousand flowers". For us, it means making one design and using it over and over, making it smaller, combining it with other canes and creating repeating patterns. Hmmm... repeating patterns.

In this book you will learn how to make several polymer clay canes. You can use these canes to make the projects in this book. You can leave the canes at the finished size stated in the cane building section or you can reduce them further. The final result is up to you and what you find pleasing. The basic procedures utilized for these canes are described here.

Roll out a length of clay 2" x 6" on the thickest setting of the pasta machine. Trim the sides and make a clean cut across the two ends.

Stacking Clay

Whenever you stack sheets of clay, care must be taken to avoid trapping air between the layers. Place a sheet of clay on top of another by starting at one end, and then pressing down, moving towards the other side. Think of it as laying wallpaper. Use an acrylic rod to fuse the sheet and remove any trapped air.

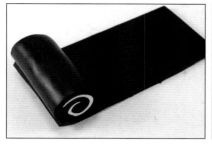  

cutting line

How to Make a Butt Joint Wrap

Roll out a sheet of clay on the desired thickness on your pasta machine. Trim the sides of the sheet to match the height of the cane to be wrapped and make a clean cut across the two ends. Place the trimmed sheet up against the cane and wrap, being careful not to trap air. • When you have wrapped the entire cylinder, roll the cylinder beyond the overlap and then roll back. • You will see that there is a slight indention in the clay marking the cutting spot for a clean butt joint.

Using your tissue blade, cut through this line. • Bring the edge against the cane. • Smooth the seam lines until they are flat.

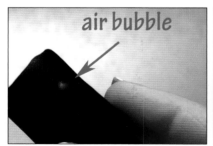  

air bubble

push air bubble up and out

slice into air bubble

Tips for Getting Rid of Air Bubbles

You can get rid of an air bubble by using your fingers and coaxing the bubble up to the edge of the cylinder. • If this doesn't work, take your tissue blade at an angle and slice into the air pocket. Use your fingers to squeeze out the air and smooth the hole.

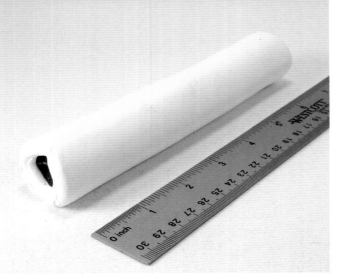

Cane Reduction

Canes come in many shapes and sizes. The design possibilities are endless because you can change the shape and sizes of your canes and combine them in numerous ways.

In order to preserve your design there are some tricks to reducing your canes.

Repeat the reduction steps working first in the middle and then working out towards the ends until you have reached the desired length and/or thickness.

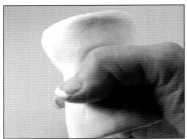   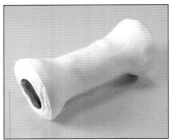

How to Reduce a Cylinder

When reducing cylindrical canes, rolling them is not a good idea because the cane has a tendency to twist. It is better to squeeze along the length of the cane rather than rolling. Start by grabbing the middle of the cane with your hand. • Squeeze gently and then turn the cane in your hands. Squeeze again. Turn, squeeze, repeat. • Work slowly. Do not squeeze too hard. Eventually, the cane will begin to resemble a bar bell, thinner in the middle and thicker at the ends.

Start working towards the ends of the cane. Squeeze, turn, repeat. Work down one end and then the other. When the cane gets a little longer you can gently pull on the ends stretching slightly. Start to gently squeeze the ends of the cane until it is the same thickness as the middle. • Work one end and then the other. • Gently roll on your work surface or between your hands, but try not to let your cane twist.

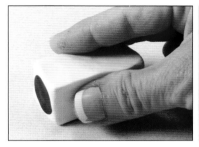  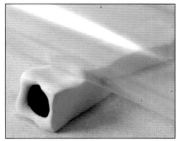

How to Reduce a Square Cane

Use your fingers to squeeze in the center of the cane. • Try to maintain the square shape and maintain uniform pressure on the cane. Just as in the cylindrical cane reduction, push down, rotate the cane and push down some more. Work out from the middle towards the end of the cane. Once the cane gets a little longer place it on your work surface. • Roll the rod or brayer along one side. Turn the cane over and repeat. Do this on all sides of the square. Flip the cane end to end and repeat.

 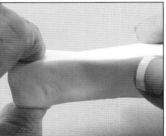 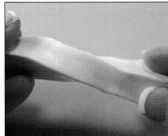 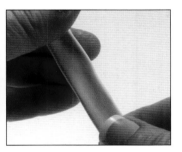

Stroke the length of your cane as if you were petting a cat. • Holding onto one end, stroke the cane. Flip the cane over. Hold onto the other end and stroke again. Repeat these steps working first in the middle and then working out towards the ends until you have reached the desired length and/or thickness. • Sometimes it helps to twist the cane as you pull gently. • Keep reducing the cane until you have reached the desired length or thickness.

Tip from the Artist

When reducing canes, you will get some distortion at the ends. When you have finished reducing your cane, cut off these distorted ends and then add them to your scrap pile. Keep cutting away the distorted end until you have the correct design showing up at both ends.

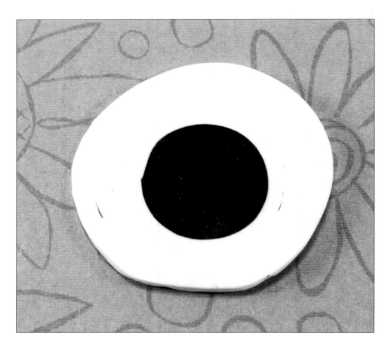

Cane #1

Bull's Eye Cane

A Bull's Eye cane is one the simplest canes you can make. It is also the building block for several canes in this book.

Roll out a length of clay 2" x 6" on the thickest setting of the pasta machine. Trim the sides and make a clean cut across the two ends.

   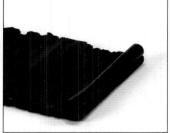

Taper both ends of the sheet using your blade or acrylic rod. • Make a thin snake cane. Using the palm of your hand, roll the clay back and forth until it is an even thickness and at least as wide as your sheet of clay. Try to be sure that there is no air in your snake. Place this snake at the start of your sheet of clay. • Press the end of your sheet up against your snake. Start rolling up your sheet of clay.

Tips for Dissecting Canes

You can create a new cane pattern by dissection. For example, if your cane is cylindrical, dissecting it in half produces two semi-circular canes.

Because it's desirable to have the same design throughout the cane, some care must be taken when dissecting. Hold the blade straight up and down to avoid angular cuts which result in one part being wider at the top, affecting the design uniformity.

Press gently as you roll so you don't cause dents in the clay. Dents cause air to be trapped in the clay. • Using the palm of your hand, roll the cylinder over your work surface until the seam is gone and the cylinder is of uniform thickness. • Trim the ends of the cylinder. This is the center of your cane. • Roll out a sheet of clay of contrasting color on the thickest setting of your pasta machine. Wrap the center using a butt joint wrap. Repeat this until the cane is approximately 2" in diameter. This will take about 5 - 6 wrappings.

Reduce this cane until it is approximately 7" long. • Trim the ends and cut into three, two inch long Bull's eye canes.

Tips for Dissecting Canes

Here are some tips for successfully dissecting your canes.
- Don't try dissecting a cane that is taller than two inches.
- Use a sharp blade.
- Make guide marks on the top and sides of your cane.
- Place the cane in front of you on your work surface. Sit up straight and position yourself so that you are looking straight down on your cane.
- Take your time. Check the blade position as you cut. Clay is very forgiving. If you go off track, take the blade out and press the clay back together. Remark your guide lines if necessary and start again.
- Try to keep the blade from curving as you slice.

Cane #2

Squared Off Bull's Eye Cane

This variation of the Bull's Eye cane is used to make the Half Moon cane and the Squiggle cane.

EXTRA SUPPLY
1" x 1" square of plastic template

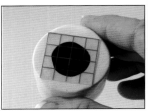

Start with a 2" cylindrical #1 Bull's Eye cane as shown on pages 24 - 25. Center a template on the top and double-check the size. Make adjustments if necessary. • If the cane is not big enough, press down with your hand until the template will fit. Do not make the cane any shorter than 1³/₄" because this may make it difficult to reduce later. If the template still won't fit, you can either add another layer of clay or make a smaller square template. • Mark the sides of the cane with your blade along the 4 corners of the square. Be sure that the mark is perpendicular to the bottom of the cane from the edge of the square to the bottom. • Do this for all four sides of the square. Look at the sides to be sure the lines are going straight up and down.

Referring to the Tips for Dissecting Canes on page 25, place your blade along one of the cutting lines on the top of your cane. Cut straight down through your cane following the marked cutting lines on the sides of your cane. Repeat for the other three sides. • You have now created a Squared off Bull's Eye Cane. Use your fingers to shape the edges of the square into sharp edges. • Using your acrylic roller can help square it off. • You have now created a Squared off Bull's Eye Cane. • To make a half cane, cut the square diagonally.
TIP: I illustrated the cane with a black center, but you can also reverse the color to make a Bull's Eye with a white center.

Cane #3

Speckled Cane

Like the 1001 dalmatians, these speckled canes have gorgeous spots. The clay in the center makes the spots, and the exterior clay creates the background color.

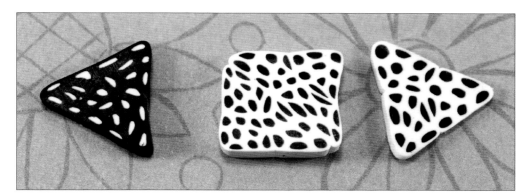

Start with a 2" Bull's Eye cane. • Reduce this cane until it is approximately ¹/₄" wide. • Cut into 1" segments.

Put all of the segments together and compress. • Do not worry if the center dots are no longer round. Reduce this cane and cut into three segments. • Rejoin the three segments into one.

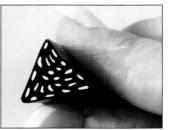

Shape the cane into a triangle. Pinch first with your fingers. • Use your work surface to further shape the triangle.

Cane #4

Dots Cane

Polka dots are a traditional favorite and a great way to fill spaces in a Zentangle. Use the entire square, or cut it on an angle to create new shapes.

Try mixing different colors such as substituting blue or red in place of the black for a patriotic color scheme.

There are many variations, so don't be afraid to experiment and have fun!

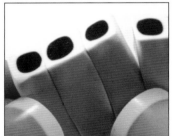

Reduce a 2" squared off Bull's Eye cane until it is ¼" wide and 16" long. Cut the cane into 1" segments. • Line up 4 segments and seal together using your acrylic roller.

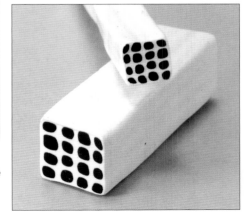

Stack 4 more segments on top and seal again with your acrylic rod. Repeat with the remaining segments. • Reduce the cane to 1" wide. • Cut a piece of the cane off and reduce to a smaller size. Now you have two canes for the price of one.

Cane #5

Striped Cane

Create distinctive striped patterns by varying the thickness of the layers or adding extra colors.

These examples show black-white-gray variations. Have fun with your canes.

 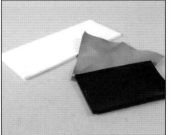  

Use white, black and gray clay. • Roll out the black on the thickest setting of your pasta machine. Cut out a sheet that is approximately 2" x 4". Roll out the gray at a thin setting. Cut out two sheets that are 2" x 4". • Sandwich the black clay between the two sheets of gray. Trim the edges. • Feed this through the pasta machine on the thickest setting.

 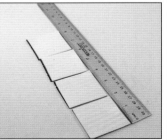  

Roll out a sheet of white clay on the thickest setting of your pasta machine. Place this on the black and gray striped sheet. Trim the edges. Feed this through the pasta machine at the thickest setting. You can stop here or, if you prefer stripes that are closer together, turn the pasta machine to a thinner setting and feed the sheet through again. • Cut this sheet into 2" segments. • Stack the segments. Use the acrylic rod to help get air out between the layers. • Cut the striped cane in half. We will use half of the cane to make another cane (see page 36).

Cane #6

Squiggles Cane

Reminiscent of puzzle pieces, there's no puzzle to putting this cane together. It's a simple process that creates a wiggly, complex, and playful pattern.

Match up

You need two 2" squared off Bull's Eye canes, one with a black center and one with a white center. Dissect each cane in half. If you made the Half Moon cane on page 39, you can use the leftover half canes. • Line up the top edge of one half circle with the bottom edge of the other half circle. • You must fill in the sides to make the cane square again by making the "missing piece". • Using one of the cane colors, roll out some clay through the pasta machine. Cut and stack the clay until it is as wide and tall as the "missing piece".

Trim the sides, top and bottom and place the stack next to the Squiggle cane to be sure it is big enough. • Place the squiggle cane on top of the stack of clay. Use a needle tool to mark the shape of the "missing piece" along the edge of the squiggle cane. • Use these marks to guide the cut to make the stack fit into the cane. • Make the top diagonal cut first.

For the second cut you will need to mark the sides and bottom with your blade. • Cut straight down following your cutting guide marks. • Place next to the Squiggle cane and check for fit. • Press into the Squiggle cane. Repeat with the other color on the other half of the cane.

  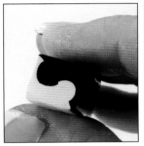 

Reduce this cane. • Cut into 4 segments. • Rejoin the four segments. • Use an acrylic rod and your fingers to smooth the seams.

Collage Clay Tip:

After reducing a cane, cut off the distorted ends until the design is no longer distorted. Add distorted ends to a scrap pile. Condition your scrap clay as needed to mix black with white to make gray.

Cane #7

Spiral Cane

Always in motion, spirals represent the eternal flow of life.

This freeform cane is so versatile... look at the variations on page 35 to see some modifications or create your own variations.

   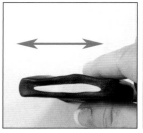 

For this cane you will need a 2" high Bull's Eye cane. • With your fingers, push in to make an oval shape. • Flatten with an acrylic rod. • Use your fingers to flatten the oval some more. • Be aware of the orientation of your cane. The oval is on the top and bottom of the cane. You want to stretch and flatten the cane such that the height of the cane remains around 2" but the oval becomes flatter and longer. • Use your acrylic rod to make the flattened oval longer.

  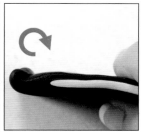  

When the cane is about 4" long, taper the ends of the cane. • Using your fingertips start to roll up the cane from one tapered end. Be careful not to get air trapped while you roll. Do not push down hard with your fingers because this will cause ridges which may trap air. You may find it easier to lay a matching clay snake across the tapered end and roll up against it. Keep in mind that this will increase the size of your center. • Using the flat of your hand, gently roll up the rest of the cane.

The Cane is cylindrical and we want a square. • Roll out a sheet of matching clay on the thickest setting of the pasta machine. Add a butt joint wrap to increase the size of the cane. • Using a square template, square off the spiral cane. • Mark the cutting guide lines on the side of the canes as you did in the Squared Off Bull's Eye cane. Cut all four sides. If you decide that there is not enough clay around the spiral you can add a wrap of clay around the cane. Run a sheet of clay at the desired thickness through the pasta machine. • Trim the sides and make a clean starting edge. • Wrap the sheet around the cane and trim at the final edge. • Use your fingers to make sharp corners on all four sides of the square.

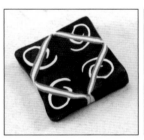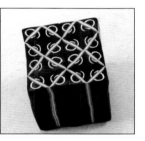

Reduce the Spiral cane that you just built until is approximately 1" wide. • Cut off a section 1" – 2" long. Dissect this section in half. • Create a clay "sandwich" that is 1 medium setting white with a thin slice of gray in either side. Place this between the two halves of the spiral cane. • Reduce this cane and cut into four sections. Recombine the sections to make a new cane. • Reduce this cane and cut into four sections. Recombine these sections to make the final cane.

Modified Spiral Canes

Cane #8
Triangle Cane

This pattern reminds me of a mosaic tile. The angles give it more eye appeal than the customary rigid right-angle design.

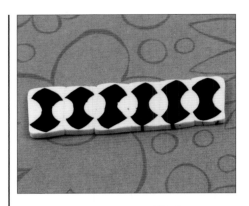

Cane #9
Picket Fence Cane

Intricate detail makes this cane look great on a project. It's easy to construct using a circle cutter.

EXTRA SUPPLY
Circle cutter

  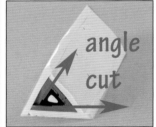

angle cut

Start with a Bull's Eye cane. Use your fingers and a table to shape it into a triangle.
• Roll out a sheet of gray clay on the thickest setting of a pasta machine. Instead of wrapping the sheet around the entire triangle, you will add gray clay to each side. Place the sheet on the table and place the triangle on top. Rest your blade along the triangle so that when you make the cut, it follows the edge of the triangle and makes an angle cut on the gray sheet. Repeat this for the other two sides. Roll out a sheet of white on the thickest setting. Cover the triangle cane as you did with the gray clay.

 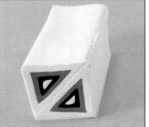

With your fingers press the edges together. Reduce the cane until it is approximately 4" long. • Cut the cane in half and rejoin the two halves. You can stop here or reduce and rejoin the cane for more variations.

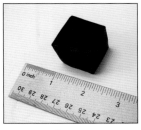    

Begin with a 1" square of black clay. • Using the circle cutter, cut straight down through the cane on one corner.
• Matching the size of the first cut, position the cutter on the opposite corner and cut down through the cane. • Place the cut out center section on top of a 1" square of white clay and use the circle cutter to mark the clay.

Cut down through the white clay along the marked line. • Return the black center piece to the top of the white clay. Use the circle cutter to mark the remaining cut. • Slice straight down through the white clay. • Exchange the black center piece with the white piece.

   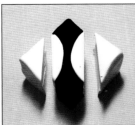 

Press the pieces together. • Align a blade with the points of the black curve as shown. • Cut straight through the white clay.
Observe the sides, being certain you don't stray into the black. • Repeat on the other side. Then, cut each side triangle into 2 pieces.

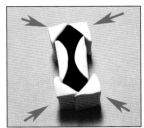 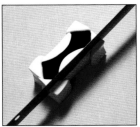   

Form a rectangle by positioning the cut triangle pieces at the corners of the center as shown. • Remove excess clay. • This is the completed cane. • Reduce this cane and then cut it into 1" segments. Rejoin the segments to make the final cane.
• Use this cane as a border in your decorated sheets. Here is a pendant I made using this cane. I used several of the canes described in this book to frame the piece.

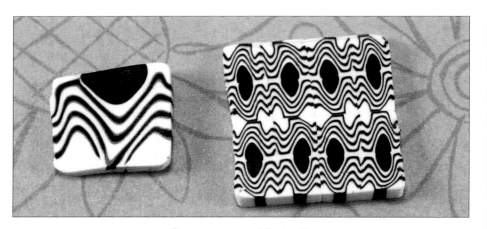

Cane #10
Curvy Lines Cane

Create curvy lines and slice off pieces to make interesting repeating patterns.

Lay 2 white snakes of clay (from page 29) across the top of the cane. Lay a snake of black clay across the bottom of cane as pictured. • Press the snakes into the striped cane and form a rectangle. • Try to eliminate any gaps. Reduce this cane.

 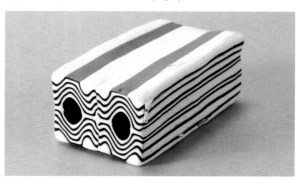

Cut the cane in half and rejoin.

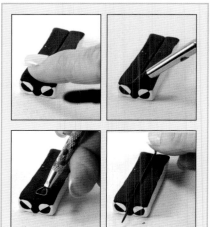

Tips from the Artist

When fitting segments together, you sometimes find a gap which must be closed to prevent holes in the centers of your canes. You can do this with your finger. • Or use a small acrylic rod, knitting needle, rubber-tipped tool or brass rod. • A clay cutting tool can sometimes cut away the gap. • Sometimes, the best remedy is to add a small snake of matching clay.

Reduce this cane until it is 8" long. Cut into four 2" segments.

Cane #11

Half Moon Cane

The patterns that emerge when canes are sliced and reassembled are truly amazing. Unexpected variations appear when the canes are assembled in a different position or with alternate colors.

 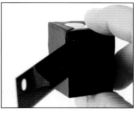 

You need two 2" squared-off Bull's Eye canes, one with a black center and one with a white center. • Dissect each cane in half. • When cutting the cane, be sure that the blade follows the edge of the cane.

Match up

We will use one of each color for this cane. The other halves can be used to make the "Squiggle Cane". Take each half and match up the center cylinder. • Match up at the bottom end first. Then slowly press together, working from the bottom to the top of the canes. Try to keep the pattern aligned and to not trap air between the canes.

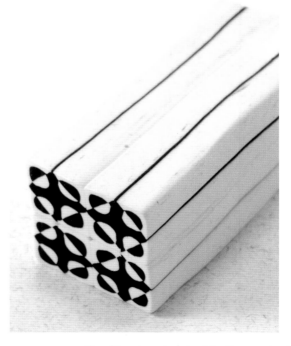

Here are 3 possible combinations for joining the 4 segments. • Choose a combination and join the 4 segments together. Be careful not to trap any air between segments. Reduce this cane, cut into 4 segments and rejoin.

Decorated Sheet

Now that you have a wonderful stack of black and white canes, you can use them to make a sheet.

Use your sheet to cover any objects that can withstand the required temperatures for baking in the oven, or make beads and boxes. The projects included in this book show just a few of the many possibilities for using decorated sheets.

EXTRA SUPPLIES
Various shape cutters
Cyanoacrylate glue
Burnisher (back of a spoon, door knob, or paper folder)

Tip from the Artist

The sheet area is divided into sections. Fill each section with a repetitive design. For these sheets you will fill each segment with a different cane pattern.

For better design, vary the design tone. For example, use some designs that are darker and some that are lighter. Use some simple designs and some that are more complex.

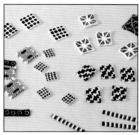

You can leave the canes the size we created or reduce the canes to shrink the size of the patterns. You can have it both ways by reducing only one end of your cane. If you want smaller slices cut from the reduced side or for a larger pattern cut from the larger end. • Run some black clay through a medium setting of your pasta machine. Trim the edges. Use a needle tool to mark off the sheet into sections. • This is only a guide and can be modified as you place your cane slices. Gather up your canes. Take thin slices off each cane and place them on a deli sheet or wax paper. • Try to make the slices the same thickness as much as possible. • Pick up the cane slices and place them on the black sheet following along the segment lines that you created. Finish a section with one cane design before moving onto the next section. When filling the next section you may have to trim some cane slices to fit.

Try not to leave gaps between the slices. • Use your fingers to smooth the seams and press the slices together. • Roll across the top of your decorated sheet. • Place a sheet of deli wrap over the decorated sheet. • Use your fingers to smooth the seams and to get rid of fingerprints.

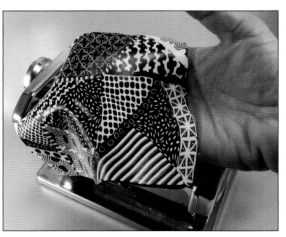

To fully integrate the cane slices you can burnish them using a rounded object such as the back of a spoon or doorknob. • With consistent pressure rub over the decorated sheet. • To obtain a uniform thickness, run the sheet through the pasta machine. Choose a thickness setting that is close to the actual thickness of your sheet to avoid too much distortion.
• You now have a completed sheet.

Big Beads

Large beads are so fashionable! You see them everywhere - in boutiques, at the mall, being worn by celebrities. Now you can create your own style and show off your love of pattern with beautiful beads that demand attention.

EXTRA SUPPLIES
1 decorated sheet
   (pages 38 - 39)
Scrap clay
Square cutter

Cut 6 squares from your decorated sheet (pages 38 - 39) for each bead using a square cutter. • Make cubes out of scrap clay that are slightly smaller than the size of the cutter used. • Place a square on each side of the cube. Be careful not to trap air under the slices. • Pinch the edges of the square together.

Smooth the gap between the edges and remove excess clay with a clay blade. • With your fingers, start pressing in the corners of the cube. • Roll the clay into a smooth, round ball. • Pierce the bead with a needle tool. If the bead is distorted during the piercing you can gently roll the bead back into a ball. • Fold a piece of heavy cardstock in an accordion fold to make a bead rack. Place the beads on the bead rack and bake according to manufacturer's instructions. Sand the beads with wet/dry sandpaper starting with 220 grit. Keep dipping the bead and the sandpaper in water. This will keep the dust down. Repeat with the other grits, 400, 600, 800 and 1000. Buff on a cloth or with a buffing wheel to get a fantastic shine.

Tip from the Artist

When piercing beads, poke through one side of the bead with your needle tool. When it is almost through to the other side remove the needle tool and poke into the bead from the opposite side. This will keep the hole looking the same from both sides of your bead.

Toggle Clasp for Rubber Cord

It's both convenient and economical to make your own matching findings. Create gorgeous toggle clasps that can't be purchased - they complement your Zentangle beads perfectly and cost next to nothing!

Once you learn to do this, you will never want to purchase another toggle again.

EXTRA SUPPLIES
Scrap of a decorated sheet (pages 38 - 39)
Rubber Cord or Buna Cord

Make a small rectangle out of clay.

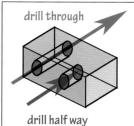
drill through
drill half way

drill half way

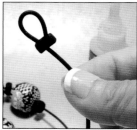

With a needle tool, pierce the rectangle to make a hole equal to the thickness of the rubber cord. You will need to make one hole that goes completely through the rectangle and one that only goes partially into the clay. • Make a bead the same way that you made the Big Beads, only smaller. Shape the bead into a football shape. Pierce the bead partially with a needle tool. Be sure that the end of the rubber cord will fit into hole. • Place the bead and rectangle onto a piece of cardstock and bake according to manufacturer's recommendations. Sand your beads with wet/dry sandpaper starting with 220 grit. Repeat with the other grits from 400 to 1000. Buff on a cloth or with a buffing wheel to get a fantastic shine. • Put a small amount of glue on one end of the rubber cord. Insert the end into the toggle bead. • String your beads or pendant onto the rubber cord. Insert the remaining end through the hole you created on the rectangle bead. Be sure to enter the bead on the side that has only one hole. Make a loop with the tubing and glue the end into the partially drilled hole. • When finished, wipe some ArmorAll onto the clay. This will help remove the white film that you sometimes get after sanding.

Pillow Beads

Here is a quick way to make beads for a beautiful bracelet.

EXTRA SUPPLIES
1 decorated sheet (pages 38 - 39)
Various size round cutters
Purchased beads with center "donut" hole
Needle • Scrimp beads • Stringing wire • Clasp

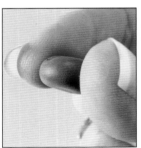

purchased bead

scrap clay

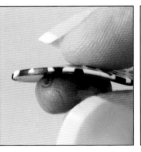

scrap clay

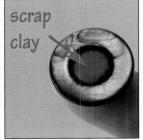

Roll out a sheet of scrap clay with your pasta machine and cut out a small circle using a cutter. Roll it into a ball and flatten slightly. • See if this size is large enough to cover the center hole of your purchased bead. If it is too small then use a larger cutter or make the sheet thicker. If it is too big, use a smaller cutter or make a thinner sheet. Once you have the correct size ball, make all of your core beads. For each pillow bead you will need a cutout of scrap clay, a cutout of your decorated sheet, a cutout of black clay for the back and a purchased bead. • Cover the front of the core bead with the cutout from the decorated sheet (pages 38 - 39). You do not need to cover the whole bead. The back of the covered bead will be hidden by black clay. Be sure that the surface is smooth and there is no trapped air in the bead. • Push the covered bead onto the purchased bead. You want to push hard enough so that the scrap clay bulges through the center hole.

   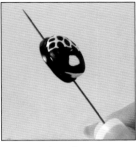 

Place a cutout of black clay over the center hole on the back of your bead. Be sure that the cutout is larger than the hole. Press together to be sure that the back piece of clay fuses with the clay from the front of the bead. • Texture the back of the bead with a hair curler. • Hold the bead on your finger. • Pierce the bead with a needle passing through the holes of the purchased bead. • TIP: Add color to a pillow bead bracelet by purchasing colored beads.

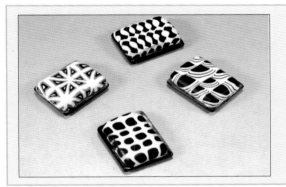

Tip from the Artist
Vary the shape and size of pillow beads.

Purchase some beads of any shape or size having an open, donut hole in the center. This is necessary for the front and back to fuse together. You will make the core of the beads out of scrap clay.

String the beads onto stringing wire. Follow the manufacturer's instructions for the scrimp beads to attach the purchased clasp and wire.

Trinket Box

Stash your stuff in style!

Create a classy treasure box for your jewelry, coins, or small craft supplies.

You can make this box in any size for a fabulous, one-of-a-kind gift!

EXTRA SUPPLIES
2 decorated sheets (pages 38 - 39)
Small screw
Texture tool (hair roller)
Corn starch or polyester batting
Cyanoacrylate glue

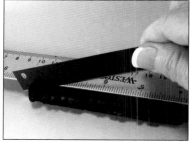

To make 4 corner posts, roll out several sheets of black on a thick setting of the pasta machine. Stack the sheets, rolling with an acrylic rod to remove air trapped between the sheets. • From this stack, cut 4 equal sized corner posts.

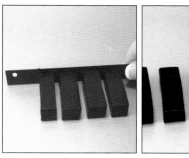    

Use a ruler to get your cuts straight. It is important that all four posts are the same height. With a texture tool, add texture to the posts. • The decorated sheets used to make the top and sides of the box need to be equal to the thickest setting of your pasta machine. If your decorated sheet is not thick enough, roll out some black clay and add it to the decorated sheet. • With a texture tool, add texture to the top and bottom of your sheets. • Cut a decorated sheet (pages 38 - 39) into four equal sides, each 1" x 4". • Place on a piece of cardstock. Place another piece of cardstock and a tile or piece of glass on top to keep the sides from curling while baking. Place the four corner posts onto cardstock. Bake according to manufacturer's recommendations. Let cool.

fill in gaps

Glue the sides of the box to the corner posts. The posts will be on the inside of the box. • Use graph paper to insure that the box remains square. • With a small paintbrush, apply Liquid Clay to each of the 4 outside seams. • If there are any gaps where the sides meet, fill with black clay. • Use your blade to remove any excess clay.

  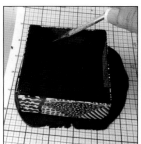 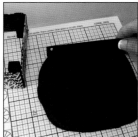 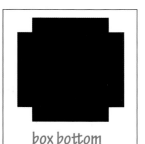

box bottom

Cut 4 pieces of black clay, each $1/2$" x $1 1/4$". • Apply one piece to each corner seam. • Cut pieces flush with sides. On the thickest setting of the pasta machine, roll out a sheet of black clay larger than your box. Place your box frame on top of the black sheet and mark the interior size with a needle tool. • Cut out the bottom of your box along the needle tool lines in a shape as shown. Place the bottom between two pieces of cardstock. Place a tile/glass on top and bake. Let cool.

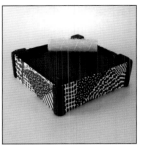

Use a small amount of glue to hold the bottom in place. If you have any large gaps between the bottom and the sides of your box, fill these with small amounts of clay. Small gaps will be covered with the two thin sheets of clay. On a thin setting of your pasta machine, roll out two sheets of black clay. The sheets need to be larger than your box. • With a small paint-brush, apply Liquid Clay to the box bottom. • Lay a thin sheet of black clay over the box bottom, starting at one side and moving to the other. Try to press down as you lay it down so that no air is trapped. If you do find you have an air pocket, press with your fingers coaxing the air pocket to the edge and out. Use a rubber tipped clay tool to gently press the clay into the corners. • With your blade or craft knife, cut away the excess clay. • Smooth the seams with your fingers or rubber tipped tool. Use your texture tool to texture the inside of the box.

decorated top sheet

Repeat this for the inside bottom of the box. Ball up a wad of polyester batting. Place the box upside down on the batting. The batting will help support the box while it bakes. An alternative to this is to bake the box on a pile of cornstarch. There would have to be enough cornstarch to fill the inside of the box. Place the batting/cornstarch and box in the oven and bake according to the manufacturer's instructions. Remove box from the oven. If the sides bend, wait until the box is cool enough to handle. While holding the sides into the correct shape, dip the side into cold water. This will "freeze" the side into its proper position. Repeat if necessary on the other sides. If the box sides are too cool and they are not straight, run the box under hot water until the sides soften up. Try the cold water technique again until the sides are straight. • Place the box on top of your second decorated sheet. Cut the top from this decorated sheet slightly larger than the box. Texture the top and the bottom of the lid with your texture tool. • Find the center of the lid using a ruler. • Use your needle tool to make a hole through the center point of the lid. Place the lid on cardstock. Bake the lid according to manufacturer's recommendations. • Roll out a sheet of black clay on the thickest setting of the pasta machine. You will use this sheet as a stopper for the inside of the lid. Cut a shape that is similar in shape to the box bottom, but smaller in size. It should fit inside of the box.

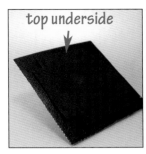

top underside

push down

When the box top has cooled, insert a small screw going from the lid bottom. • Apply Liquid Clay on the bottom side of the lid. Remember that the inside stopper is smaller than the lid so don't apply the Liquid all the way to the edge. • Place the inside stopper sheet on the bottom of the box lid. This will cover the screw. Texture the stopper sheet. Apply a small amount of Liquid Clay to the screw that is exposed on the lid top. • Take a small ball of black clay and push it onto the screw.
• Push the clay down on the screw until it meets with the lid of the box. • Try to be sure that the clay is tight up against the screw. Add a football shaped bead of black clay onto the screw. • Place the lid on batting or cornstarch and bake.

Julie Eakes

Julie is an award-winning polymer clay artist. She loves the challenge of making complex canes and is known for her fabulous face canes. Julie is a popular teacher and enjoys taking workshops. Find out more about this amazing artist and view more of her work at **JulieEakes.blogspot.com**.

Suppliers - Most craft and variety stores carry an excellent assortment of supplies. If you need something special, ask your local store to contact the following companies:

ZENTANGLE
www.zentangle.com offers resources, Zentangle kits, supplies, a list of certified teachers, information on workshops, news, and a gallery of projects.

ZENTANGLE BOOKS
DESIGN ORIGINALS
www.d-originals.com

KATO CLAY, LIQUID CLAY SEALER & TOOLS
Kato Clay, www.vanaken.com

PREMO CLAY
Sculpey, www.sculpey.com

FIMO CLASSIC CLAY
www.staedtler.ca

PHOTOEZ, STENCILPRO SILK SCREEN
Circuit Bridge, www.cbridge.com

PERMANENT PIGMA MICRON® 01 PENS
Sakura, www.sakuraofamerica.com

FINE SHARPIE® PENS
Sharpie, www.sharpie.com

PAPERCON DELI WRAP, PLASTIC WRAP
www.cooking.com

MANY THANKS to my staff for their cheerful help and wonderful ideas!
Kathy Mason • Kristy Krouse
Janet Long • Donna Kinsey

Big Big Beads

If big isn't big enough for you, try making these Big Big beads. Or in this case, one nice sized pendant.

EXTRA SUPPLIES
1 decorated sheet (pages 38 - 39)
Glass ornament
Round cutter
Cyanoacrylate glue
Small drill

Tip from the Artist
When fusing unbaked clay to baked clay, brush on a little Liquid Clay. This will help make the bond stronger.